Fifty Favorite Birds
Coloring Book

Lisa Bonforte

Dover Publications, Inc.

New York

Publisher's Note

The fifty species of birds assembled in this book are commonly occurring examples that can be seen in or quite near cities and towns in many or most parts of the United States (not including Hawaii) and Canada. They have been rendered for your coloring pleasure by the artist Lisa Bonforte, who has also provided color versions on the covers of this book as a guide for identification and accurate coloring. The birds shown are adult males unless otherwise specified.

Ms. Bonforte has based her drawings on the paintings by Bob Hines in *Fifty Birds of Town and City*, a booklet published in 1978 by the U.S. Department of the Interior Fish and Wildlife Service (editors: Bob Hines and Peter A. Anastasi).

In the present volume, the captions give the common and scientific names of the birds and the seasons and ranges in which they occur in the United States and Canada.

Published in Canada by General Publishing Company, Ltd., 30 Lesmill Road, Don Mills, Toronto, Ontario.

Published in the United Kingdom by Constable and Company, Ltd., 10 Orange Street, London WC2H 7EG.

Fifty Favorite Birds Coloring Book is a new work, first published by Dover Publications, Inc., in 1982. See Publisher's Note for further details.

DOVER *Pictorial Archive* SERIES

International Standard Book Number: 0-486-24261-7

Manufactured in the United States of America
Dover Publications, Inc.
180 Varick Street
New York, N.Y. 10014

BALTIMORE ORIOLE (*Icterus galbula*). Male above, female below. Found in summer in southeastern Canada and eastern two-thirds of the U.S.

BARN SWALLOW (*Hirundo rustica*). Found in summer throughout U.S. and western Canada.

BLACK-CAPPED CHICKADEE *(Parus atricapillus)*. Found year-round in northern half of U.S. and western Canada.

EASTERN BLUEBIRD *(Sialia sialis).* Summer: southeastern Canada, northeastern and north central U.S. Year-round: southeastern and south central U.S.

BLUE JAY *(Cyanocitta cristata)*. Found year-round in eastern two-thirds of U.S. and southeastern Canada.

BOBWHITE (*Colinus virginianus*). Male standing, female with chicks.
Found year-round in eastern two-thirds (excluding northernmost states)
and northwestern corner of U.S.

LEFT: WHITE-BREASTED NUTHATCH *(Sitta carolinensis)*. Year-round through most of U.S. RIGHT: BROWN CREEPER *(Certhia familiaris)*. Summer: southern and western Canada, northern U.S. Winter: eastern two-thirds of U.S. (excluding northernmost states). Year-round: western U.S. and parts of Northeast.

BROWN THRASHER *(Toxostoma rufum)*. Summer: northeastern and north central U.S. Year-round: southeastern U.S.

CANADA GOOSE *(Branta canadensis)*. Winter: southern and western U.S. Migrant throughout U.S. in spring and fall.

CARDINAL *(Richmondena cardinalis)*. Female left, male right. Year-round in most parts of the U.S.

CATBIRD *(Dumetella carolinensis)*. Summer: most of U.S. except West
Coast. Winter: extreme southeastern U.S.

CEDAR WAXWING *(Bombycilla cedrorum)*. Male left, female right. Summer: southern Canada and far northern U.S. Winter: southern half of U.S. Year-round: northeastern and north central U.S.

CHIMNEY SWIFT *(Chaetura pelagica)*. Found in summer in eastern half of U.S.

CHIPPING SPARROW *(Spizella passerina)*. Summer: most of Canada
and U.S. Year-round: southeastern and southwestern U.S.

COWBIRD (Eastern Cowbird; Brown-headed Cowbird; *Molothrus ater*).
Female left, male right. Summer: western Canada and northern half of U.S.
Year-round: most of southern half of U.S.

COMMON CROW *(Corvus brachyrhynchos)*. Summer: most of Canada.
Year-round: most of U.S.

16

DOWNY WOODPECKER *(Dendrocopus pubescens)*. Female left, male right. Year-round in most of U.S. and wooded parts of Canada.

FLICKER *(Colaptes auratus).* Summer: most of Canada. Year-round:
generally, eastern half of U.S.

GOLDFINCH (Common Goldfinch; American Goldfinch; *Spinus tristis*).
Female in center, others male. Found throughout U.S. with seasonal range
variation.

GRACKLE (Common Grackle; Purple Grackle; *Quiscalus quiscula*). Summer: most of southern Canada and northern U.S. Year-round: southeastern quadrant of U.S.

GREEN HERON *(Butorides virescens)*. Found in summer in eastern half of U.S.

HERRING GULL *(Larus argentatus)*. Summer: Canadian far north. Winter: North American coasts. Migrant throughout U.S. and Canada.

HOUSE SPARROW *(Passer domesticus)*. Male left, others female. Year-round throughout U.S. and southern Canada.

HOUSE WREN (*Troglodytes aedon*). Summer: most of U.S. Winter: Gulf
Coast and part of southwestern U.S.

SLATE-COLORED JUNCO *(Junco hyemalis)*. Male in foreground, female in background. Summer: most of Canada. Winter: most of U.S.

ABOVE: KILLDEER *(Charadrius vociferus)*. Summer: southern Canada and northern U.S. Year-round: southern U.S. BELOW: MALLARD *(Anas platyrhynchos)*. Female in foreground, male in background. Summer: most of Canada. Winter: most of U.S.

MOCKINGBIRD (*Mimus polyglottos*). Year-round in most of U.S. except northwestern and north central states.

MOURNING DOVE *(Zenaidura macroura)*. Year-round in most of U.S.

MYRTLE WARBLER (*Dendroica coronata*). Male above, female below. Summer: most of Canada. Winter: generally, southern U.S. Found as migrant in most of U.S.

BELOW: NIGHTHAWK (*Chordeiles minor*). Found in summer throughout
U.S. and Canada. ABOVE: TURKEY VULTURE (*Cathartes aura*). Summer: northern U.S. Year-round: southern U.S.

30

PIGEON *(Columba livia)*. Year-round throughout U.S. and in much of
Canada.

PURPLE MARTIN *(Progne subis).* Found in summer in most of U.S.

RED-EYED VIREO *(Vireo olivaceus)*. Found in summer in much of Canada and most of U.S. (not Southwest).

RED-HEADED WOODPECKER (*Melanerpes erythrocephalus*). Summer: north central U.S. Year-round: most of eastern U.S.

RED-WINGED BLACKBIRD *(Agelaius phoeniceus)*. Male above, others female. Summer: most of Canada and U.S. Year-round: southern half of U.S.

ABOVE: ROBIN *(Turdus migratorius)*. Summer: most of Canada. Year-round: most of U.S. BELOW: WOOD THRUSH *(Hyclocichla mustelina)*. Found in summer in eastern half of U.S.

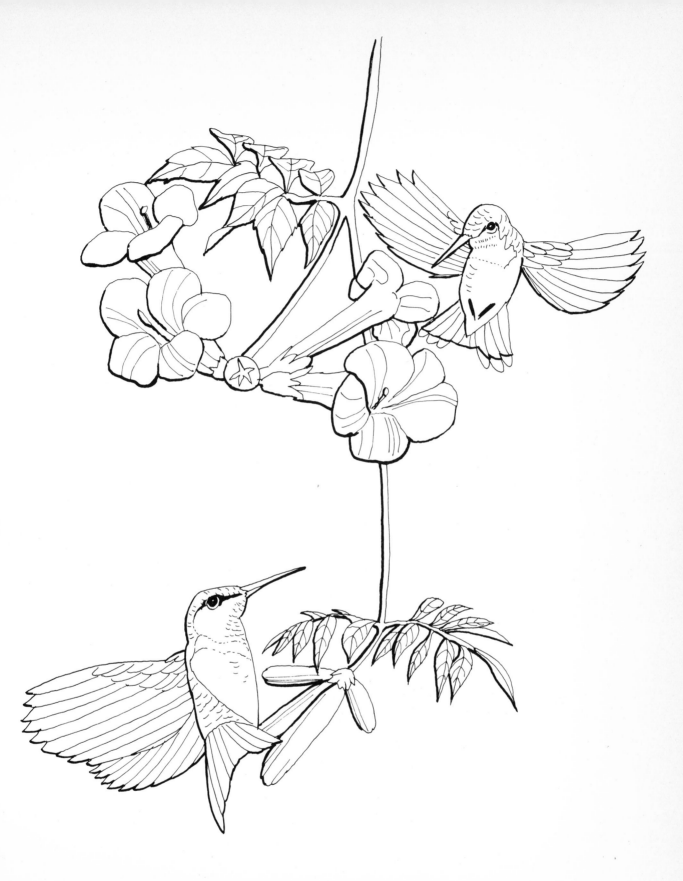

RUBY-THROATED HUMMINGBIRD (*Archilochus colubris*). Male left, female right. Found in summer in eastern half of U.S.

SONG SPARROW *(Melospiza melodia)*. Summer: most of Canada. Winter: southern U.S. Year-round: northern U.S.

SPARROW HAWK *(Falco sparverius)*. Summer: most of Canada, northern
U.S. Year-round: southern U.S. and West Coast.

STARLING *(Sturnus vulgaris)*. Summer: southern Canada. Year-round: throughout U.S.

TOWHEE *(Pipilo erythrophthalmus)*. Male above, female below. Found in most of the U.S. most of the year.

TUFTED TITMOUSE *(Parus bicolor)*. Found year-round in eastern half of the U.S.

WHITE-CROWNED SPARROW *(Zonotrichia leucophrys)*. Summer: northern and western Canada. Winter: southern U.S. Year-round: U.S. West Coast and west central states. Migrant in eastern Canada and northeastern U.S.

EASTERN WOOD PEWEE *(Contopus virens)*. Found in summer in eastern half of U.S. and parts of southeastern Canada.

44

YELLOWTHROAT *(Geothlypis trichas)*. Male above, female below. Summer: most of Canada and U.S. Year-round: southernmost states of U.S.

YELLOW WARBLER *(Dendroica petechia)*. Found in summer in most of
Canada and U.S.